D1560361

F. Remy Diederich

LifeChange Publishing

Starting Over:
finding God's forgiveness when
you find it hard to forgive yourself
Copyright © 2017
F. Remy Diederich

ISBN -13: 978-1542387507
ISBN-10: 1542387507

BISAC: Religion/Christian Ministry/Counseling & Recovery

For Jodi,
and everyone like her,
who find it hard to believe
that God loves them so much.

CONTENTS

Introduction

THIS IS A SHORT BOOK. That's intentional. Surprisingly, many people never read to the end of a book. They have good intentions, but life happens.

This is a book I want you to finish. It's too important not to finish. You can have this read in an hour or two. But if you read a little bit each day, over twenty days, you might get more out of it since it will have more time to soak in. You decide. Whichever way will enable you to finish the book, do that.

My hope is that reading this book will be like hitting the reset button on your computer. We've all had it happen: you have so many programs running that the computer freezes up. You sit there frustrated, staring blankly at the screen, not knowing what to do. It finally dawns on you to power down and reboot. You hit reset, and voila! You are on your way again.

Maybe that's what you need personally. A reset. A do-over. A clean slate. Call it what you will; it's a chance to start over. Thankfully, God offers you just that. It's his gift to you. He knows you are made of dust. He knew you'd need a do-over even before he created you, so he put a plan in place to reclaim your broken life. It's your chance to hit the "reset" button.

Before you think it's too good to be true, read the book. It won't take long, and it could change your life.

F. Remy Diederich

Day One: Throwing it All Away

TIME MAGAZINE REPORTED the reemergence of Eliot Spitzer, the former governor of New York.[1] He was known as a man who fought corruption with a vengeance only to be exposed as a regular user of a high dollar prostitution ring. To make matters worse, he covered his addiction by sending money to shell corporations that funneled the money back to the prostitution ring. TIME called it,

> *...hypocrisy on a scale that was hard to fathom...as if Eliot Ness had been busted for peddling gin from his apartment.[2]*

When the news hit the paper, Spitzer's career was over. Currently he is trying to find his way back into politics, but the writer of the story wasn't so sure it could happen. She said,

> *To learn that Spitzer was the world's biggest hypocrite, that he'd thrown it all away to frequent prostitutes, was devastating, a lapse that could never be forgiven.*

When she mentioned this to Spitzer, he responded,

> *"'How do you think I feel?'... his eyes welling up. 'At one point, I stood for something that was important and useful. I was in a place in time where I had a purpose, where it mattered. And then I destroyed it.'"*

Thankfully his wife seemed to forgive him but not without some residue in their relationship. The article said,

His wife...appears to have forgiven him. "I don't know if you can ever mend something like this, in the sense of repair the canvas so that you never see the tear in the fabric," he said. "I'm incredibly lucky to be with a woman who is willing to deal with that tear in the fabric and keep moving forward."

Spitzer said there would always be a scar in the fabric of his marriage. TIME said the public would never be able to forgive him. And Spitzer himself said he destroyed his purpose in life.

As I read this, it made me wonder if Spitzer will be defined by his indiscretion for the rest of his life. Will his name be synonymous with hypocrisy and prostitution forever? Will he ever be able to move beyond his mistakes or the shame?

I wonder the same thing about Tiger Woods. His multiple indiscretions sank his marriage and sent his golf career in a downward spiral. Will he ever be able to move beyond his affairs and be seen as a man of integrity again? Or will his affairs define him for the rest of his life? Will he always be known as the greatest golfer...who never was?

I don't want to pick on these men. That's not my intention. They are easy targets for critics. Their failures have been well documented in the press. I only bring them up because I'm concerned for those of us who – like Spitzer and Woods – have a past that overshadows our present and future.

Maybe you have also made mistakes, or suffered failures, that haunt you and rob you of the life that God planned for you. Can you imagine hitting the "reset" button on your life? How would that change things for you?

God has good things in store for you. He wants to help you start over. That's what I want to explore over the next few pages. Let's work at getting your life back.

Day Two: Starting Over

ONE OF JESUS' FOLLOWERS told a story about a woman that might give us some perspective on what it takes to start your life over. She was caught in the act of adultery and shamefully dragged to the center of the temple court where the religious elders surrounded her. Disgusted with what she had done, they planned to stone her to death.

In that culture, her sin defined her. Adultery made her worthless and disposable. But just before the first stone was launched, Jesus stopped the men and said,

> *If any one of you is without sin,*
> *let him be the first to throw a stone at her.*

Slowly the men dropped their stones and walked away: each one aware of his own sin. Then, after the men left, Jesus turned to the woman and said,

> *"Woman, where are they? Has no one condemned you?"*
> *'No one, sir,' she said. "Then neither do I condemn you...*
> *"Go now and leave your life of sin."*
> John 8:10,11

Jesus refused to define this woman by her sin. He refused to assess her value based on her weakest and most shameful moments. There was more to her than that. Instead, Jesus forgave her, giving her hope of a new life beyond adultery. He chose to recognize the dignity that God granted her at birth so she could start over.

If Jesus were to sit down with Eliot Spitzer today, I don't think he'd spend much time talking about the sins of his past. I think he'd spend more time talking about the hope of his future and the potential that he has. That's the nature of forgiveness. Forgiveness doesn't dwell on the past. Guilt, condemnation, and punishment all dwell on the past. Forgiveness cleanses us from our past and looks to the future.

If you are struggling with guilt today, I want to encourage you that you have a future. God hasn't given up on you. Forgiveness frees you to start over.

Day Three: But I Don't Feel Forgiven

MANY PEOPLE WRESTLE with not feeling forgiven. They might know intellectually that God forgives them (because of what they've been told), but they don't *feel* forgiven. It doesn't seem real to them: just wishful thinking.

I spoke with a woman once about her faith. I asked her if she believed that God forgave her, and she said she did. Then I asked her if she thought she would go to heaven when she died, and she said she wasn't sure.

When I asked the woman why that was, she said, "Well, I'm just not sure if I'm good enough. I'm not sure that I've done all that God wants me to do." I replied, "I can answer that for you. Absolutely not. You've failed miserably!" But then I added with a smile, "We've all failed miserably. That's why we need a Savior."

None of us could ever be good enough to live up to the standards of a perfect God. Thankfully, God doesn't forgive us because our good deeds outweigh the bad ones. We are forgiven because of what God has done for us.

To put it another way: God doesn't welcome us into heaven because we did everything right. He welcomes us into heaven because *he's* done everything right. He's done for us what we are unable to do for ourselves.

I told this woman that it's like the strongman challenge at the county fair where you hit a lever with a sledge-hammer and it shoots a puck up to try to ring a bell at the top of the pole. We are like the proverbial hundred-pound weakling who wants to win a stuffed animal for his girlfriend. He keeps swinging and swinging, but the puck never even gets close to ringing the bell.

Our attempts to earn forgiveness, or a relationship with God, are truly pathetic! We'll never be good enough to "ring the bell" on our own. But Jesus stands up in our place and rings the bell with one swing. He doesn't just ring the bell; he blows the bell right off the pole. He does what we could never do on our own. As a result, we win the prize. But the prize isn't a stuffed animal; it's a relationship with God and the abundant life that flows out of that relationship.

The mistake that many of us make, when it comes to our guilt, is that we focus on our weakness and not on God's strength. We focus on our inadequacy and not God's sufficiency. When you shift your focus, from yourself to God, everything changes.

Day Four: Stop Punishing Yourself

WHY ARE WE SO QUICK to dwell on our failure? I think it's because we feel the need to punish ourselves for what we've done. Rather than embrace God's forgiveness and celebrate it, we embrace guilt as our cross to bear: our penalty for failing God.

We know we can't make things right. We can't undo our past or fix what's broken. But maybe if we embrace guilt God will see our remorse and be pleased with us. We hope that embracing guilt will salve our regret and soften God's judgment against us.

That's our solution...as bad as it is. But God has a better solution. He forgives us. I know that might sound simplistic; the apostle Paul put it like this:

> *God was reconciling the world to himself in Christ,*
> **not counting people's sins** *against them.*
> 2 Corinthians 5:19 (emphasis mine)

That's such a simple definition of forgiveness: *not counting your sins against you*. Paul compares God to an accountant checking his books with its debts and credits. In God's "ledger book" you have no outstanding debts. You don't have to worry about getting harassing "collection calls" because Jesus paid all your debts with God.

Why would God cancel what you owe him? The first part of that verse explains why: God was reconciling the world to himself. You can't bring two people together if they are both pointing out each other's faults. Forgiveness is necessary for reconciliation to take place. Since God's goal was to connect with his people, forgiveness became the requisite means to achieve that goal.

Do you see how failing to forgive yourself works against God's plan? God doesn't want you rehashing your mistakes and beating yourself up over them. That's why he canceled your debt. He wants you to accept his gift of forgiveness so you can be restored to him and live a new life. If God isn't counting your sin against you, it makes no sense that you try to pay him back.

The best thing you can do is agree with his ledger. It reads "PAID IN FULL." Believe it and then live like you believe it.

Day Five: Jesus Dealt With Your Sin

YOUR PAST CAN HAUNT YOU. God understands that until you deal with your past you'll never have a future: you'll never experience the wholeness you long for. The problem is, you can't do anything about your past. There's no going back. If you have any hope it must come from outside of yourself. That's why Jesus dealt with your past for you.

There's a letter in the Bible that was written to primarily Jewish believers. Jewish believers grew up with a religious system that offered animal sacrifices to "pay" for their sin. So the writer of this letter used the metaphor of sacrifice to help his readers understand what Jesus did. He said that Jesus:

> *...appeared once for all...to do away with sin by*
> *the sacrifice of himself.*
> Hebrews 9:26

To "do away" with your sin means that Jesus eliminated it. He destroyed it. Sin no longer has any power over you. It can't be held against you. Because of this, you are free from your past. It's as if your sinful behavior never happened. You are free to live your life without constantly looking over your shoulder, waiting for God's judgment to catch up with you.

Now, you might still have to pay the consequences of your sin. If you are in debt $100K, you will still need to pay that back. But God's not holding your sin against you. He's not trying to sabotage your life to get back at you, or withhold his relationship from you until the debt is paid. On the contrary, like the woman caught in adultery, he offers you a new life immediately: a new life in relationship with him.

Plan B, C, D...

You might say, "Remy, you don't understand. It's too late for me. I messed up so bad. I will never be who God wanted me to be. I'm sure I'm the last person God wants in his family." If these are your thoughts, you are thinking too small! You think that God only has one plan for your life and you blew that plan. You are thinking there is only Plan A and, if you mess up Plan A, there's no Plan B.

Let me tell you, when you mess up, God has Plan B waiting. And when you mess up Plan B, Plan C is next. You might be living Plan Z right now, and you think for sure that you've run out of options. You feel like you are pushing your luck with God, that God's fed up with you and ready to wash his hands of you. But guess what? God has other alphabets for you!

I'm not encouraging you to use every alphabet in the universe! I just want you to understand that God's forgiveness never runs dry. You can't out-sin God's forgiveness.

Don't give up on yourself. God hasn't.

Day Six: The Role of Repentance

THE BIBLE CONTAINS A SIGNIFICANT amount of writing from a doctor by the name of Luke. Luke traveled with the apostle Paul and wrote two books. He wrote a book about Jesus that we call the Gospel of Luke. And he wrote the book of Acts, which tells the story of the early church.

It's clear from Luke's perspective that Jesus' mission on earth was wrapped around securing our forgiveness. Let me trace some of Luke's writing about God's forgiveness.

In the very first chapter of his book about Jesus, Luke told us about John the Baptist, the prophet that came announcing Jesus. He said that John the Baptist came:

> *...to give God's people the knowledge of salvation*
> *through the forgiveness of their sins...*
> Luke 1:77

The word salvation means to be "rescued from a threat." So, look at that sentence. What's the threat mentioned? It's sin. Sin is a threat to our relationship with God. The guilt of sin weighs us down and convinces us that we are far from God.

What has the power to save us from the threat of sin? God's forgiveness. Forget all the self-help books you've read. If you haven't found God's forgiveness, the guilt from sin will eat away at you at some level. God's forgiveness is your salvation.

Now, let me show you four more verses from Luke's writing that relate to forgiveness. See if you can find what they all have in common. Luke told us about the ministry of John the Baptist. He said that John:

...went into all the country around the Jordan, preaching a baptism of repentance for the forgiveness of sins.
Luke 3:3

And then, before Jesus left the Earth, he made reference to the role of the messiah:

... repentance for the forgiveness of sins will be preached in his name to all nations, beginning at Jerusalem.
Luke 24:47

Luke told us how this happens when Peter preached his first sermon saying:

Repent and be baptized, every one of you, in the name of Jesus Christ for the forgiveness of your sins.
Acts 2:38

And then again, Peter (referring to Jesus) told the Jewish leaders that:

God exalted him to his own right hand as Prince and Savior that he might give repentance and forgiveness of sins to Israel.
Acts 5:31

What do these verses all have in common? Forgiveness is linked to repentance. Repentance is a fancy word for changing the way you live and changing your mind about God.

Now, be careful how you interpret the connection between repentance and forgiveness. People often make the mistake of thinking that we repent – or change – in order to be forgiven. The truth is; we repent *because* we've been forgiven. Starting over is possible when we believe that we have a clean slate.

I'll look at the connection between forgiveness and repentance in the next chapter.

Day Seven: Which Comes First...
Repentance or Forgiveness?

SOME PEOPLE CHANGE THEIR BEHAVIOR in hopes of being forgiven. But others change their behavior because they *have been* forgiven. Consider two examples.

Imagine that you've offended me, and you want to restore our relationship. So, in example number one, I say to you: *If you change, I'll forgive you.* That seems fair enough. But how does that make you feel? It feels very conditional doesn't it?

The first thing you think is: *How much do I need to change in order to be forgiven? Can I change just a little? Or do I need to change a lot? Does Remy expect perfection? What if I don't change enough? What if I can't change? Is it worth it?*

You see, when I lay down conditions, you stop concentrating on our relationship and you start concentrating on your behavior. The more you focus on your behavior, the worse it gets. And then you start to worry about what I think. *Is Remy happy with me or mad at me? Does he think I'm working hard enough, or does he think I don't care?* It all gets very unhealthy, very fast. You might even give up on the relationship out of shear frustration.

Now, consider example number two: You offend me, but I forgive you completely. I promise not to hold anything against you. Period. No strings attached. You may have lost my trust, but I'm not out for revenge or to withhold my kindness. How does that feel? Pretty good, doesn't it?

Instead of dwelling on past failure, my forgiveness looks to the future. No guilt. No wondering if you are working hard enough. My forgiveness gives you hope that our relationship can be restored.[3]

Because you have hope, you are more willing to change your behavior. You are free to leave your past and make a fresh start in our relationship. Your repentance (change) flows out of my forgiveness, not the other way around.

That's exactly how God wants his forgiveness to impact you. He wants his forgiveness to draw you into a relationship with him and give you hope for a future. In fact, the apostle Paul told the church in Rome that:

> *...God's kindness is intended to lead you to repentance.*
> Romans 2:4

Repentance *follows* God's kindness. God's kindness compels us to change our behavior.

Author Dean Merrill put it like this:
> It's only natural to assume that in...ministry to the fallen, repentance comes first. The sin of the past must be confronted and confessed in order to restore oneself to a holy God and release his blessings in the future.

Theologically, that is impeccable. Psychologically, it doesn't work very well...The opening task in ministering to those who have made a major mistake in their lives is to restore confidence. It is to let them know that God just might accept them again in spite of what has transpired. It is to light the match of hope, to crack the gloom.[4]

If you want to draw close to God, work at fully understanding the depth of God's forgiveness first. Once you grasp God's forgiveness, changing your behavior will be much easier.

Day Eight: The Benefits of Forgiveness

GOD SENT JESUS INTO THE WORLD to deal with our failure. The Bible refers to our failure as "sin." Dealing with our sin cost Jesus his life. If you gave your life for something, you'd hate for your sacrifice to go to waste. So, you can imagine how passionate God must be to have everyone receive the forgiveness that Jesus' death bought us.

There are countless benefits of forgiveness, but let me give you just three here.

You Can Connect With God

First, forgiveness enables you to connect with God. It does that by removing every obstacle between you and God. When God looks at you he doesn't see your past like you do. He's aware of it, but it's not a deal-breaker. There are more important things to focus on. God wants to focus on who you will become, not who you were.

You Are Perfect In God's Eyes

Second, forgiveness makes you perfect in God's eyes. That might sound too good to be true. I had it explained to me like this. Imagine that you and Jesus are sitting side by side and Jesus asks Father God: *Which one of us is more perfect in your sight?* What would the Father say? He'd say, *"You are both perfect in my sight."*

When I first heard this, it sounded wrong. How could I be equally perfect in God's sight as Jesus? But that's what Jesus' death did for you and me. The Bible tells us:

> By one sacrifice God has **made perfect**
> forever those who are being made holy.
> Hebrews 10:14 (emphasis mine)

This verse is about you. Jesus' death made you perfect in God's eyes: not for a moment, but forever. It tells you that Jesus' death cleaned your slate.

When my kids were little and they first started doing the dishes, I'd often have to go back and rewash them because they missed some spots. Our forgiveness is a lot like that. It's spotty. It's not often complete. But God's forgiveness is perfect. The word "perfect" means "to be fully complete. Nothing lacking." God doesn't miss a spot when he cleanses you from your sin. As a result, you stand before God completely blameless.

When is the last time someone looked at you as completely blameless? Wouldn't it be nice to have someone look at you without remembering all of your mistakes, all your sin, all your failure, and past history? That's how God looks at you.

But the really good news is that this cleansing isn't a temporary state. It doesn't have a thirty-day shelf life. This cleansing lasts...*forever*. That means you can breathe deep. Relax. Quit looking over your shoulder. Your struggle is over. You've been restored to God and he is now in the process of making you "holy," that is, set apart for his purposes.

I started the book talking about Eliot Spitzer and his public disgrace. Do you think Mr. Spitzer would like someone to look at him and see nothing but perfection instead of the biggest hypocrite in New York? I bet he would. I bet he'd be willing to pay large sums of money to be seen as perfect if he could. But he doesn't have to pay anything for it. Jesus already paid the price. It's his for free.

What about you? What would it be like to know that you stand before God blameless? Do you think that would bring healing to your soul?

You've Been Made New

The third benefit of forgiveness is that it makes you completely new. Elliot Spitzer may never again have anyone on earth look at him as a "new man," but the Bible says that God sees him that way... if he is in Christ.

If anyone is in Christ, – that is, a believer and a follower of Jesus – *the new creation has come: The old has gone, the new is here!*
2 Corinthians 5:17

That's a great promise, isn't it? That's what happens when God forgives you. Your old life is buried and you are resurrected to start your life over. Forgiveness pushes the "reset" button on your life.

Would you like to start over? Are you tired of carrying a load of guilt and feeling stuck in your past? How would you like to let go of your past in exchange for a new life? If so, then consider praying this prayer:

Father...thank you that you don't let my past failures define me. You define my life by your Son. You said that if I am in Christ I am a new person. I share his perfection. What a promise! What a hope! Help me to let go of my old life and embrace my new identity. Help me receive every bit of forgiveness that Jesus' death purchased for me and nothing less. And help me to live out this new life every day. Amen.

Take Time to Reflect

YOU'VE BEEN READING for a bit now. Take a moment to read through these questions to help you process what you've learned so far.

1. What are your thoughts about Eliot Spitzer and Tiger Woods? Do you think they will always be defined by their indiscretions?

2. What will it take for them to regain their integrity?

3. On the continuum that goes from "Rarely feel guilty" to "Always feel guilty," where do you fall? Why do you think that is?

4. Why is it that some people can know intellectually that they are forgiven but still not feel forgiven?

5. How is a person impacted by experiencing God's forgiveness? In other words, what does life look like for a person who has experienced God's forgiveness compared to a person that hasn't?

6. Do you think you will go to heaven when you die? Why or why not?

7. Do you agree that forgiveness comes before repentance? Why or why not?

8. Do you agree that believers are as perfect as Jesus? Why or why not?

Day Nine: The Problem of Guilt

LET ME TELL YOU ABOUT STEVE. Steve has a drinking problem, but he never saw it coming. He got started drinking heavily in college with his buddies. He thought after college that things would change, but he found that old habits die hard. Steve realized that he didn't have the self-control he thought he had.

When Steve's friends invited him to the bar, he always said yes. When they encouraged him to have one more, he never said no. After the third drink, he lost count. He knew it wasn't right, but thought, "Hey, I'm not hurting anyone." He was just having a good time.

In his honest moments, Steve knew that he *was* hurting someone. His drinking hurt his health. It hurt his relationships. It hurt his job performance. It also hurt his relationship with God, not because of his behavior, but because of Steve's guilt. His guilt pushed him from God.

Steve wanted to change, but things had gotten out of control, and he didn't know how to get back on track. Like I said: he never planned his life to be this way. One thing just led to another.

Interestingly enough, Steve's faith in God was actually a part of the problem. He felt so ashamed of his failure that he drank more to try and cover his guilt. It was a vicious cycle. The more he drank the guiltier he felt. The guiltier he felt the more he drank.

After a while, Steve stopped feeling guilty. He grew numb. He just accepted the fact that he was a drinker and resigned himself to a life without God. It wasn't what he wanted, but it was better than feeling guilty all the time.

Steve's story describes many people I've talked to over the years. Just change the name, and the addiction, and Steve might be someone you know. Steve might even be you. Instead of a drinking problem it might be a problem with food, pornography, gambling, shopping, anger, or any number of things.

What often keeps us from getting the help we need is guilt. We are so ashamed of what we've done that we push God away, assuming he wants nothing to do with us. But in doing that, we push away our greatest help.

What if Steve could live a life free from guilt? How do you think Steve's life would change if he knew that he was completely forgiven, and God accepted him unconditionally, just the way he was... warts, addiction, and all?

More importantly, how would *your* life change if *you* knew that you were completely forgiven and accepted unconditionally?

I'm not talking about being free from all guilt. Some guilt is good. True guilt helps you to recognize when you've done something wrong and helps you to take ownership of the problem. That's a good thing. I'm talking about the false guilt that lingers and often turns to shame. I'm talking about the feeling that weighs on you and makes you want to avoid anything remotely associated with God because you are convinced of his disgust for you.

True guilt has a short shelf life. What I mean is that once guilt serves its purpose in getting you to see your wrong, it starts to spoil if you hang onto it. It's like milk: if you hang onto it too long it turns sour. In the same way, guilt turns from being helpful to being hurtful.

But many people keep drinking the "sour milk" of guilt thinking it's the right thing to do... even the godly thing to do. They just assume that all guilt is from God and so they embrace it. Big mistake.

The truth is that God wants your guilt to move you to his grace as quickly as possible. Put your past behind you and start building your new regret-free life.

Day Ten: Let God Throw You a Party

I'VE BEEN MAKING THE CASE that when you go astray, God's first priority isn't to get your behavior back in line. God's not nearly as concerned about your behavior as you might think he is. God's first priority is to reestablish your relationship with him. He wants to eliminate your guilt so you will feel free to draw close to him.

If you were to graph it out, there is an inverse relationship between guilt and your relationship to God. When guilt increases, intimacy with God decreases. When guilt decreases, intimacy with God can soar. That's why receiving God's forgiveness is so important. Forgiveness removes the barrier of guilt that we erect, keeping us from God.

The Prodigal Son

You might know the story of the prodigal son that Jesus told: the son that ran away from home but finally decided to return after sowing his wild oats. The shock of that story is that the boy didn't return to an angry dad who punished him for his behavior like you'd expect. The boy returned to a dad that met him at the gate of the city with a hug, a kiss, a ring, and his favorite cloak. Then he threw his son a party.

Jesus used that story to teach us how God thinks about sin and guilt. Most dads would not greet their runaway son with a party! But God isn't like most dads. He's much more interested in his relationship to you than he is in getting you to obey a list of rules.

That doesn't mean God doesn't care about rules. They have their place. It's just not the first thing on his mind. The first thing on God's mind is restoring relationship with you. Once that relationship is established, then he can help you with your behavior.

Most dads wouldn't be as humble as the Prodigal's father was. Most dads would feel like their son dishonored them and feel the need to "teach them a lesson." But God wasn't concerned about reputation. He was more concerned about *restoration*. In order to make that happen the Bible tells us that Jesus humbled himself in the form of a servant, even to the point of dying on a cross. (See Philippians 2)

When God looked at us and saw the impact of sin and guilt on our lives, he must have said... *If I don't deal with their sin and guilt they'll always be on the run from me.* That was unacceptable to him and so God laid out a plan to deal with our sin. Let's see what that was.

Day Eleven: A Strange Solution

NO ONE COULD EVER GUESS God's solution to the sin problem. One New Testament writer put it like this:

Without the shedding of blood there is no forgiveness of sin.
Hebrews 9:22

Say what? Indulge me here. Most people won't take the time to talk about this because it seems too weird, even offensive. They don't want to scare people away from God by talking about blood. But if you are serious about finding God's forgiveness, you should know the full story. It will help settle the issue for you once and for all.

It's true: you and I will never be forgiven without the shedding of blood. What does that mean? Well, that concept goes way back to the earliest part of the Bible where Cain and Abel brought an offering to God (Genesis 4). God accepted the offering of a sacrificed animal (where there was blood) but not the offering of grain. Genesis doesn't teach on this point. It just tells the story and we are left to interpret its meaning.

As we continue reading in the Bible we start to see a theology develop in regard to the importance of shed blood. In the book of Leviticus, God articulates the importance of animal sacrifice.

If someone brings a lamb as their sin offering, ... They are to... slaughter it for a sin offering...Then the priest will take some of the blood of the sin offering...and put it on the horns of the altar...and pour out the rest of the blood at the base of the altar.

In this way the priest will make atonement ... for the sin they have committed, and they will be forgiven.
Leviticus 4:32-35

I don't know what you think of that. The idea that God requires a blood sacrifice in order for us to be forgiven seems violent, archaic, and even barbaric, doesn't it? That's bothered me at times. I've heard people say... *Look, God is God. He sets the rules so why does he require a sacrifice to forgive sin? Why can't he just forgive us without this silly shedding of blood?*

But I have to think that God hears a question like that and says: *With all due respect, you have no idea what you are talking about when you question blood sacrifice. You see the world as it is and think that it's basically good with a few flaws. But I remember the world as it was in the beginning and it sickens me what has happened to it. Humanity has done violence to my creation. Violence ruined my creation and only a violent act of sacrifice will heal it.*

So, even though blood sacrifice seems brutal and barbaric to me, I have to trust that God knows what he is doing. He knows that without the shedding of blood, there is no forgiveness. Somehow in the cosmic mystery of how God wove his creation together, he chose to incorporate the shedding of blood as a requirement for forgiveness. I accept that. I hope you will too.

Day Twelve: Right Idea. Wrong Lamb.

GOD LAID OUT AN ELABORATE SYSTEM of blood sacrifice in the Old Testament that Jews followed for a couple thousand years. Then their temple was destroyed by the Romans in 70 A.D. But surprisingly, the book of Hebrews tells us that the Old Testament sacrificial system never actually removed the guilt of sin. The system pointed to the need for something greater than animal sacrifice.

> ... the gifts and sacrifices being offered **were not able**
> to clear the conscience of the worshiper.
> Hebrews 9:9 (emphasis mine)

The writer is saying: We've been offering sacrifices for centuries, but we all know that these rituals never took care of our guilt. They never cleared our conscience and gave us peace. They never removed the barriers of guilt and unworthiness that we put up, convinced we were a disappointment to God. Sacrificing animals failed at bringing us close to God.

In fact, it says in the next chapter of Hebrews that the sacrifices actually *added to* their sense of guilt by being a constant reminder of their sin:

> But those sacrifices are an annual reminder of sins. **It is impossible**
> for the blood of bulls and goats to take away sins.
> Hebrews10:3,4 (emphasis mine)

The purpose of the Jewish system wasn't to deal with sin. The purpose of the sacrificial system was to point out the problem of sin and that a sacrifice for sin was necessary to solve the problem. But clearly, animal sacrifice wasn't the answer. God had something better in mind to take away our sins, once and for all.

Day Thirteen: Religion Isn't the Answer

THE OLD TESTAMENT SYSTEM of animal sacrifice was inadequate to cleanse us from our sin and restore us to God. Let me explain with a little more detail. (To follow along with what I am about to describe, do a Google search for Old Testament Tabernacle).

Old Testament priests would sacrifice a lamb and then bring the blood of the lamb into a place called the Holy of Holies. This is where God's presence resided. It was separated from the Holy Place by a thick curtain.

Inside the Holy of Holies was a golden box called the Ark of the Covenant. Two golden angels were attached atop the box and faced each other. The space between the angels was considered the throne of God, often referred to as the "mercy seat." Once a year, the High Priest would bring the blood of a sacrificed lamb into this place and sprinkle it on the mercy seat to seek God's forgiveness for all people.

But, do you see a problem with this system? One person got to be in the presence of God for a few brief moments once a year.

That's not a relationship. That's a visit.

And so, as we saw in chapter twelve, as long as this elaborate system was in place, and it must be repeated over and over, it only proved that there was no true forgiveness. A better answer was still out there. Rather than drawing people close to God, this system kept people at a distance from God.

This is a good picture of most religion. Most religions have some kind of process, or ritual, that addresses sin. But the focus is more on sin than forgiveness. You walk away more conscious of how bad you are, rather than how close you are to God. You leave feeling just as far from God as when you came, maybe even farther.

I remember as a kid having to go to confession in the Catholic Church. Now, I'm not trying to pick on Catholics. So, don't get me wrong. I'm just telling you my personal experience. My experience with confession was always more about guilt than obtaining forgiveness and drawing close to God. Maybe you can relate.

I had to make sure I had my list of sins in hand so I wouldn't forget what I had done wrong. And then I had to tell the priest my sins. That was scary. You walk into this dark booth where the priest sits hidden behind a screen.

It's all very intimidating for a ten-year-old boy. Then the priest gave me my penance, which was always a list of prayers to pray. I never understood why they used prayer for punishment. I'm sure it was never meant to be that, but that's how it came across, and that's how my family always talked about it.

The worse your sins were, the more prayers you had to pray and the more times you had to pray them. It was all so negative. I never walked away feeling cleansed or free because of my confession. I never felt closer to God or thankful for God's mercy and grace. I was just relieved that I survived the ordeal, and it bought me more time until the next time I had to do it.

Again, I'm not trying to pick on Catholics. Similar things happen in all kinds of churches all the time. But my experience is a good example of how religion doesn't deal with our guilt. Religion often adds more guilt. There has to be a better answer.

Day Fourteen: Once and For All

THE LETTER TO THE HEBREWS sets Jesus' sacrifice apart in stark contrast to the ineffectiveness of the religious system of animal sacrifice. In contrast to the Jewish priests it says that Jesus:

> *...is able to **save completely** those who come to God through him,*
> *...Such a high priest **meets our need**...Unlike the other high priests, he*
> *does not need to offer sacrifices day after day, first for his own sins,*
> *and then for the sins of the people. He sacrificed for*
> *their sins **once for all** when he offered himself.*
> Hebrews 7:25-27 (emphasis mine)

Let's take a look at these verses. First it says that Jesus is able to save us *completely*. That means totally, with nothing lacking. Jesus doesn't just bring us half way to God. He doesn't just forgive most of our sin. He forgives us completely.

When Jesus died, he didn't leave any fragment of sin on the table. He died for every last speck of sin, even the scent of sin that might hang in the air so that when God looks at you, what he sees, and even smells about you, is perfect. Can you believe that?

I mentioned earlier that Hebrews says, *"...by one sacrifice God has made perfect forever those who are being made holy"* (Hebrews 10:14). I know some people struggle with the idea that God sees them as perfect. But... *that's the good news!* That's the power of forgiveness. That's the miracle of salvation.

That's why the old-time hymns talk about the "power of the blood" because it's the blood that is shed for our forgiveness. That's why we celebrate Good Friday. If God just saw us as barely acceptable, that's not good news. That's nothing to get excited about.

The good news is that Jesus saved you completely from every stupid, arrogant, pathetic, immoral, shameful, and embarrassing thing that you ever did. And he gives you a fresh start every day, along with his Spirit, to give you the power to live a new life instead of a retread of your old life.

The text in Hebrews 7 continues to say that Jesus didn't have to offer a sacrifice over and over like the other priests did. He did it *once and for all*. There aren't many things in life that we do just once. We typically have to do things over and over again because nothing lasts forever. We paint our houses every few years. We have to keep repairing our cars, and we buy new clothes. Everything on earth wears out and needs replenishing.

But Jesus' sacrifice was so effective that he only had to do it once. This idea is repeated again a little more emphatically in chapter ten.

> ***Day after day*** *every priest stands and performs his religious duties;* ***again and again*** *he offers the same sacrifices, which can never take away sins. But when this priest (Jesus) had offered for all time* ***one sacrifice*** *for sins,* ***he sat down*** *at the right hand of God...*
> Hebrews 10:11,12 (emphasis mine)

A priest never sat down until his job was done. So, when Jesus sat down, it communicated that his work was finished: his job was over. His work was so perfect that he could sit down, confident that there was nothing more to do. Jesus' sacrifice was able to take away our sin when the other sacrifices couldn't.

I hope you see how this relates to you. The fact that Jesus sacrificed once and sat down means that not only has every sin of your past been paid for, but every sin that you'll ever commit in the future has also been paid for. You don't have to ever wonder, or worry, if Jesus took care of your sin. Jesus sacrificed once and for all... that is for all sin and for all people.

Day Fifteen: Don't Resurrect Your Sin

THE BIBLE OFTEN PORTRAYS JESUS as the true sacrificial lamb. When John the Baptist saw Jesus, he said...

> *Look, the lamb of God who **takes away the sins** of the world.*
> John 1:29 (emphasis mine)

What did Jesus do with your sin? He took it away. There's that phrase again. Do you remember what it said in Hebrews: *the priests weren't able to take away the sins?* But when John saw Jesus he said, *this is who we've been looking for! He's the missing link! He's the one that will finally take our sins away.*

Paul used this same phrase in his letter to the Colossian church:

> *When you were dead in your sins and in ... your sinful nature, God made you alive with Christ. He forgave us all our sins, having canceled the charge of our legal indebtedness, which stood against us and condemned us; he has **taken it away**, nailing it to the cross.*
> Colossians 2:13,14 (emphasis mine)

Jesus took your sin away and put it to death. Jesus wasn't the only one who died on his cross. Your sin died too. It was eliminated. And when sin is gone, guilt evaporates. Right?

If you still feel guilty, in spite of your knowing what Jesus did, then you have some kind of disconnect. Something is blocking your emotions from experiencing the relief of what Jesus has done for you.

Some people continue to experience guilt because forgiveness sounds too good to be true. They refuse to let Jesus take away their sin and insist on punishing themselves. They might momentarily experience the relief of God's forgiveness but they keep dragging their sin back. They think they are doing God a favor by obsessing over their failures.

Have you ever had a dog that dragged things back? You would throw something gross away but he would always find it and bring it back home? You might try to outsmart your dog by burying whatever it was you wanted to hide from him. But he couldn't be fooled! He'd sniff and dig and discover where you buried it. Then he'd drag it back to your door, or worse, into your living room. The crazy thing was, the dog was so proud of what he did. He sat there looking for praise and you were like, *What are you doing? Get that out of here!*

That's what some people do with their sin. They resurrect it over and over again! And strangely, they take some kind of spiritual pride in it, thinking they are showing God their deep repentance. Their lives revolve around their past sin and regret instead of revolving around thanking God for taking away their sin.

Do you do that? God wants you to let it go. Jesus has taken your sin and nailed it to his cross. It's time to stop punishing yourself and start living your life in thanksgiving to God for all that he's done. Living life forgiven is a much better reflection on God than if you live your life feeling guilty.

Take Time to Reflect

BEFORE YOU MOVE ON to the final part of this book, take time to reflect on the questions below. I hope they help you to meditate on the forgiveness that Jesus won for you.

1. Think about a time when you thought you'd save some money and do the work that you should have hired a professional to do. (If not you, someone you know). How did that work for you? Compare this to you trying to do the work of God in regard to your forgiveness.

2. I talked about Steve's problem with drinking. Have you, or someone you've observed, ever been trapped in the cycle where your guilt only pushed you (or them) deeper into sin? Describe it.

3. In the story of the Prodigal Son, the son's sin pushed him so low that he finally came back to his father. Read Luke 15:20-24. What characterized the homecoming of the boy? That is, what did the father do to receive him back? How does this relate to God's attitude toward you?

4. Read Hebrews 9:6-9. Inadequate religion doesn't cleanse the conscience. Think about the inadequacies of the sacrificial system. How do other religions inadequately deal with sin?

5. Read Hebrews 7:23-27, 9:11-14, 10:11-18. Compare the work of Jesus to Jewish priests. Note as many differences as you can.

6. I mentioned that sin has brought violence to God's creation and therefore sin requires a violent solution. What are your thoughts about the fact that God requires the shedding of blood to secure our forgiveness? Is it really necessary?

7. Hebrews emphasizes the fact that Jesus died "once and for all." What is the significance of this phrase to you?

8. Hebrews 8:1 and 10:12 say that Jesus "sat down" after making his sacrifice. What is the significance of his sitting down? (confer verses 10:17 and 18)

Chapter Sixteen: You Are Worth It

I DON'T KNOW IF YOU'VE ever thought about it this way, but Jesus' death and resurrection are all about God's love for you: his intense passion for you. They are about his desire to reconnect with you in a personal way.

How does it feel to know that you are the object of God's love? It's as if you have a target on our back and God is coming after you, but he's not coming to get you, or judge you, but to embrace you ... if you'll let him.

This relationship is made possible because God forgave you. But forgiveness came at a price. Like I explained earlier, the Bible tells us that there is no forgiveness without the shedding of blood. And so, God stepped up and said, "I'll pay that price."

What was the price God paid to forgive you? Peter said it well:

*It was not with perishable things such as silver or gold that you were ransomed from the empty way of life handed down to you from your ancestors, but with **the precious blood of Christ,** a lamb without blemish or defect.* (emphasis mine)
1 Peter 1:18,19

If the value of something is graded on the price paid, then how valuable are you to God if the price paid for you was the blood of his only Son? This verse tells me that you and I are of infinite worth to God and no one can take that away from us.

Let Me Get That

Have you ever been in the process of paying for a meal and someone said, "Let me get that"? That's what God did. He knew we couldn't afford to pay for our sin. He knew that it wasn't in our power to restore our relationship to God, and so he said, "Let me get that."

God's great love for you motivated him to forgive you. When Jesus entered Jerusalem the week of his death, he came for your forgiveness. When he prayed in the Garden of Gethsemane, and sweat blood, he did it to obtain your forgiveness. When he was beaten until his back ripped open, it was for your forgiveness. When nails were driven through his hands and feet, and he hung on a cross until he died, it was for your forgiveness. And when Jesus rose from the dead it proved that he succeeded in obtaining your forgiveness!

Jesus was obsessed with obtaining your forgiveness and he did it gladly. The writer to the Hebrews said:

For the joy set before him he endured the cross.
Hebrews 12:2

What was the joy set before him? You are God's joy. You are what motivated him to endure the cross. He did it all so you could be restored to a relationship with him. Can you believe that? Isn't that amazing? And God thinks that you are totally worth every drop of blood that Jesus spilled.

Being in a daily relationship with you is God's joy. And it's fair to say that *not* being in a daily relationship with you is his sadness. Jesus took your sins and gave you the right to know God personally: to call him "friend" and "Father." There is nothing keeping you from God. There's no bouncer at his door. Jesus' death made a way into God's presence for you and everyone on the planet.

The only obstacle keeping you from God is you. It's up to you to enter into the relationship that Jesus made possible for us all.

Day Seventeen: Forgiveness is a Call to Action

I'VE SHARED THIS VERSE TWICE NOW, but let me share it one more time:

By one sacrifice he has made perfect forever those
who are being made holy.
Hebrews 10:14

That's a powerful statement of forgiveness. Jesus' death made us perfect in God's eyes. But forgiveness does more than deal with your past. Forgiveness deals with your future.

Jesus died for not only your past sins but every sin in your future. That's what it means when it says that we were made perfect FOREVER. That means your good standing with God never changes no matter what you do.

But that's not all that God does. If you look at the second part of this verse it tells you that God has a plan for your life. He wants to make you holy.

Now, you might not be so sure you want to be made holy! That might sound pretty boring to you. You're afraid that you'll have to start wearing a long robe and chant, go on silent retreats, take a vow of poverty, and avoid any appearance of fun.

Well, don't worry. That's not what it means to be made holy. To be made holy means that God helps you to shift your focus from living to please yourself to living to please him. The word "holy" means to be set apart for God.

Experiencing God's forgiveness should change your life. It's never been exemplified better than in the musical, *Les Miserables*. The story is about an ex-convict by the name of Jean Valjean. He's just gotten out of prison and he has nowhere to live. He resorts to asking the local bishop if he can stay with him.

The bishop welcomes Jean Valjean into his home for the evening. But the temptations prove to be too much for him. Jean Valjean steals the bishop's silverware, knocking him down as he runs away. The next day the police catch Jean Valjean and return him to the bishop.

Jean Valjean was like many of us. He was defined by his past; filled with guilt and regret. He even had a certificate that documented his crime and branded him as a criminal for life. He feared he would never again be known for who he was or who he might become. He'd always be known for what he had done. It was dehumanizing. As a result, he quit trying to be good. He didn't blink at stealing from a priest. In his mind, he was a documented loser. He chose to become the person that people thought he was.

But the bishop was determined to help Jean Valjean see his potential. That required Jean Valjean to experience forgiveness…first. The bishop didn't just forgive him and allow him to keep the silverware. He blessed Valjean by offering him two silver candlesticks that he left behind. And then he said:

Jean Valjean, my brother, you no longer belong to evil, but to good. It is your soul that I buy from you; I withdraw it from black thoughts and the spirit of perdition, and I give it to God.[5]

What was he saying? He was saying: *My forgiveness has set you free from your past so you can live the life God meant for you to live.* The priest said this hoping that his forgiveness would lead to Jean Valjean living a changed life.

That's exactly what Jean Valjean did: changed his life. He changed his identity, moved to a new town, and became a successful businessman, as well as the mayor of the town. But more importantly, he was a blessing to those around him. He adopted a troubled girl. He rescued people from death. He fought injustice, and he forgave his archenemy. He lived the new life that the priest called him to live. That's the power of forgiveness.

For Jean Valjean, forgiveness wasn't a gift that he passively remembered with half-hearted appreciation. Forgiveness was a call to action. It was a call to live a new life.

This story isn't just for the stage. It's for you and me to live out every day. If Jean Valjean turned his life around over the gift of two candlesticks, how much more ought we to change our lives for the price that was paid for our forgiveness? Let me requote the apostle Peter:

It was not with perishable things such as silver or gold that you were ransomed ... but with the precious blood of Christ, a lamb without blemish or defect.
1 Peter 1:18,19

The price paid for us not only shows our worth but also the level of gratitude from which we ought to live our lives. Or as the apostle Paul told the Christians in Corinth:

You were bought with a price, therefore honor God with your bodies.
1 Corinthians 6:20

Jesus gave his life for us. It only makes sense that we would give our lives to him in return.

Day Eighteen: Living Forgiven

LET ME ASK YOU A QUESTION: if you believe you've been forgiven, then how has forgiveness changed you? How are you different because of God's forgiveness? Jesus didn't forgive you to simply relieve your guilty conscience so you could sleep better at night. He forgave you so you could know God and live the life you were created to live.

The church has made a mistake by proclaiming God's forgiveness without asking for a response. Forgiveness is free, but if we truly understand what God did for us, it should change everything.

Pastor and author Timothy Keller said this about Martin Luther and the purpose of faith:

> Luther so persistently expounded... "We are saved by faith alone, but not by faith which is alone." That is, we are saved, not by anything we do, but by grace. Yet if we have truly understood and believed the gospel it will change what we do and how we live. [6]

The Impact of Forgiveness

Over the next few days, I want to share four ways that forgiveness can impact the way you live. We'll continue to look at the letter to the Hebrews.

The writer takes ten chapters to carefully explain why Jesus' death paid for our sins, enabling God to forgive us and restore us. Then he tells us how being forgiven should impact us. It says:

Let us draw near to God with a sincere heart in full assurance of faith, having our hearts sprinkled to cleanse us from a guilty conscience and having our bodies washed with pure water.
Hebrews 10:22

This verse tells us the first way that forgiveness changes you: forgiveness lets you draw near to God. It says that we don't just have "assurance" but we have "full" assurance. Adding the word "full" in front of "assurance" means that God has left no room for doubt.

Jesus' sacrifice was so perfect that you can be absolutely confident that God accepts you, no matter what you've done in your past: not because you have perfect faith, or have lived the perfect life, but because Jesus was the perfect sacrifice. When you have that confidence, you are free to approach God and start your life over.

Keep reading to learn the other ways forgiveness impacts you.

Day Nineteen: Living Forgiven (continued)

THE SECOND WAY FORGIVENESS changes your life is it helps you to hold onto your faith. Hebrews says:

> *Let us hold unswervingly to the hope we profess,*
> *for he who promised is faithful.*
> Hebrews 10:23

Do you have a faith that comes and goes with your emotions or your life experiences? When things are good you have faith, but when things are bad your faith goes out the window. But the writer is saying:

Look, once you understand what Jesus did for you there should be no more question about where you stand with God. You don't have to avoid God when you've been bad and reappear after you've been good for a while. He accepts you unconditionally.

Every once in a while, I'll run into someone who used to be a part of Cedarbrook (where I serve as pastor) and I'll say, *Hey, what's up? Good to see you.* I'm just being friendly and letting them know that I missed them.

But most often, they'll immediately look sheepish and start telling me why they haven't been in church.
They tell me how life went south on them. They got laid off, or they had a relationship fail; they were struggling with an addiction, or there was some big disappointment in their life and so they dropped out of church. And my response is...

Your life doesn't have to be perfect to engage at church. We are a bunch of broken sinners doing our best to encourage each other to follow Jesus.

Why do people fall away at the time they need God the most? Their guilt is what often keeps them away. They don't understand that Jesus' sacrifice has made them perfect forever in God's eyes and therefore they are always welcome. There is no shame. When they return to church the church should receive them like the Prodigal's father received his son: with no accusations but a party.

If you fear that your sin has made you unacceptable, let me tell you, you never have to worry about that with God. As Dean Merrill said in the article I quoted earlier, God is unshockable. Nothing fazes God. He's seen it all! That's why Hebrews adds in verse 23: "for he who promised is faithful." That means that God's not going to let go of you just because you messed up. He's faithful. Like Paul told Timothy...

> *If we are unfaithful, he remains faithful,*
> *for he cannot deny who he is.*
> 2 Timothy 2:13, New Living Translation

If God won't let go of you, there's no reason to let go of him.

Maybe you've been away from God for a while. Reading this book might be your first step back toward God in months or even years. God would say to you: *I'm glad you're back, but now I want you to stay. Don't give up on me because I haven't given up on you.*

Day Twenty: Living Forgiven (continued)

THE THIRD IMPACT THAT FORGIVENESS should have on your life is to move you to love and good deeds.

Let us consider how we may spur one another on toward love and good deeds, not giving up meeting together, as some are in the habit of doing, but encouraging one another...
Hebrews 10:24,25

Like Jean Valjean, a forgiven person stops living for himself, or herself, and starts to help others. We can't accomplish this on our own. God wants us to work with other believers. This kind of interdependent community is what's called the church.

Church is much more than a Sunday meeting. Church is a community of believers committed to love and good deeds. At least it should be. If you are serious about your faith, don't avoid meeting with other believers. Keep seeking out opportunities to join other believers to subversively plot how to love others and do good deeds.

The final impact forgiveness has is that forgiven people change their ways:

*If we deliberately **keep on sinning** after we have received the knowledge of the truth, no sacrifice for sins is left, ...*
Hebrews 10:26,27 (emphasis mine)

In other words: Jesus didn't forgive you so you could keep on sinning. He forgave you so you could live a new life. And Jesus sent his Spirit into your life so you have the power to live that new life. Paul told the Roman church:

If the Spirit of Him who raised Jesus from the dead is living in you, He who raised Christ Jesus from the dead will also give life to your mortal bodies because of His Spirit who lives in you.
Romans 8:11

This means that the Spirit of God comes to give you the power you need to become the person that God called you to be. The Spirit of God is pure and holy, so it's actually quite shocking that he can come into our lives. But this is possible because Jesus cleansed us with his forgiveness.

You No Longer Belong to Evil
Do you remember what the priest said to Jean Valjean? He said "you no longer belong to evil." Forgiveness breaks the power of evil and sets you on a new trajectory. The apostle Peter put it this way...

But you are a chosen people, a royal priesthood, a holy nation, God's special possession, that you may declare the praises of him who called you out of darkness into his wonderful light.
1 Peter 2:9

God's calling on everyone is to show people the goodness of God. Whether you realize it or not, that is what God made you for. That's why God forgave you and raised Jesus from the grave... so you could live a life that shows the world the goodness of God.

Imagine if everyone took the priest's charge to Jean Valjean as their personal challenge. What would the impact be if we all chose to abandon our past and live a life of love and good deeds?

Take Time to Reflect

1. Can you think of a time when someone paid for you when you couldn't afford to on your own? When was that and how did it feel?

2. It's been said that Jesus would have died for you alone if you were the only one on earth. Do you believe that? How would it feel to watch Jesus die knowing that he was doing it just for you?

3. Read Hebrews 10:14. What does it mean to be made holy? How can you be perfect AND be in the process of being made holy?

4. Do you agree that forgiveness is a call to action? Why or why not? Confer 1 Corinthians 6:20

5. What stood out to you the most about God's forgiveness as you read this book? What do you want to make sure you remember? How will it change your life?

Conclusion: Receiving God's Forgiveness

I'VE LEARNED SOMETHING after working with hundreds of people on spiritual matters: there's nothing I can do, or say, to convince people to believe. There is no iron-clad, slam-dunk argument that eliminates all questions or compels people to follow my teaching. So, I realize that after laying out my reasons for why God has forgiven you, you may still not feel forgiven or believe it's true.

It's as if I've laid a big package in front of you and described the wonderful contents. But I can't make you open the package and enjoy the gift. That's up to you. Will you open the package? Or maybe ask God to help you open it?

Remember, it's a gift. The apostle Paul put it like this:

> *...it is by grace you have been saved, through faith—*
> *and this is not from yourselves, it is the gift of God.*
> Ephesians 2:8

You don't deserve a gift. You can't earn gifts or pay for the ones you receive. You simply accept gifts and offer thanks for them. I hope you will do that now and start your life over.

Let me close out our time together with a prayer:

Father, thank you for my reader. Thank you that they are concerned enough about finding your forgiveness that they picked up this book. You know their heart. You know their hesitations and fears. Please help them to remove the barriers that prevent them from believing in you and your forgiveness. Help them to understand your amazing unconditional love. Might they lay hold of your forgiveness in a way that empowers them to hit the "reset" button on their life and start over. Might they be transformed to generously love and serve others so that you will get all the praise. Amen.

Did you find this book helpful?
Would you let others know?

Please take a minute to rate this book on Amazon.com and leave a brief review. It will help others find the book and encourage them to read it. Thanks so much.

Would you like this book to be available at your church?
You can purchase these books at a discount at
www.createspace.com/6841690
Use discount code: ZJRYS5AH for 25% discount.

Other Books by F. Remy Diederich

Healing the Hurts of Your Past...*a guide to overcoming the pain of shame.* In this practical guide, Remy breaks down what causes our insecurities and shows how they manifest in a variety of self-destructive ways. But unlike most self-help books, Remy goes beyond describing the problem; he offers a solution by clearly helping the reader find their infinite worth from knowing God.

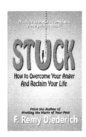

STUCK...*how to overcome anger and reclaim your life.* Anger is natural. It's a God-given gift to process loss. With this positive approach to anger, Remy walks his reader through a deeper understanding of what causes anger and how to process it effectively. This process involves a discussion of grief, loss, and forgiveness. Remy's practical approach enables his reader to work their way through complex life scenarios to free themselves from feeling STUCK in anger.

Return From Exile...*overcoming loss, failure, and personal setbacks.* Few people recognize their loss and fewer people understand the devastating impact it can have on them. In this forty-day devotional, Remy walks the person through the experience of loss using the metaphor of exile. He explores the pain of it, but also explores how God can use loss to transform you and prepare you for the next phase of your life.

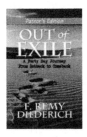

Out of Exile: Pastor's Edition. This book is directed at helping pastors and ministry leaders who have suffered a setback in ministry and are looking to make a comeback. It formed the basis for "Return from Exile."

Broken Trust: *a recovery guide for survivors of spiritual abuse, toxic faith, and bad church experiences.* Too many people are hurt by their church experience. It was never meant to be that way. Rather, the church was meant to offer hope to the world. In this practical guide, Remy helps you determine the next steps you might take to recover from your experience and hopefully return to a healthy church.

ACKNOWLEDGMENTS

I'm grateful for the many people that have honestly shared with me their fear of not being forgiven. I hope God will use this book to settle the question once and for all.

I want to thank my wife, Lisa, for her help with not only this book but in critiquing much of my work before it reaches the masses. I try not to run everything by her, but when I'm not sure I'm making much sense, I turn to her for clarity. Thank you dear for your help!

I also want to thank Jason Brooks for his unselfish help in getting my writing career off the ground. He is always willing to give me the help I need and offers great graphic and marketing advice. Plus, he makes me laugh and I need that. Thanks Jason.

And finally, I want to thank the growing team of people that read my books in advance to offer feedback and eventually promote the book. You give me a lot of confidence that my writing will hit the target. (If you would like to join this team, please contact me.)

ABOUT THE AUTHOR

F. Remy Diederich is the founding pastor of Cedarbrook Church in Menomonie, Wisconsin and serves as the Spirituality Consultant to Arbor Place Treatment Center. He is married with three adult children.

VISIT: www.readingremy.com

Facebook: F. Remy Diederich
Twitter: @FRemy

END NOTES

[1] *Eliot Spitzer's Impossible Mission*, by Sheelah Kolhatkar, March 15, 2010, TIME.

[2] Elliot Ness was the leader of the famed "Untouchable" crime squad that fought bootleggers during Prohibition.

[3] Just to be clear, I'm not talking about trust. Trust and forgiveness are not the same. I can forgive you immediately. But trust takes time. They don't always go together.

[4] *After the Fiasco: Restoring Fallen Christians*, Dean Merrill, Christianity Today. Copyright 1989.

[5] *Les Miserables*, Victor Hugo, Chapter 12

[6] Timothy Keller, forward to *Dietrich Bonhoeffer*, by Eric Metaxas

Made in the USA
Coppell, TX
16 April 2022

76690987R00046